Braids & Bows

Anne Akers Johnson & Robin Stoneking

Principal Photography
Peter Fox
Thomas Heinser
Jock McDonald

Additional Photography
David Peterson
Kim Gilbert Raftery
Ed Young

Art Direction
MaryEllen Podgorski

Design
Jacobs Fulton Design Group

Illustration
Sara Boore

Book Production
Elizabeth Buchanan
Jill Turney

Inspiration
Darrell and Nan

Printed in Singapore. Ornaments
and box, China and Taiwan.

Write Us.
Klutz Press is an independent
publisher located in Palo Alto,
California and staffed entirely
by real human beings. We would
love to hear your comments
regarding this or any of our books
(a complete catalogue is
available through the mail).
Klutz Press/2121 Staunton Court/
Palo Alto, CA 94306.

Table of Contents

Taking Care of Your Hair

Washing

For clean, healthy hair, it's a good idea to wash it 3 or 4 times a week. Always wash your hair after you swim.

Start by brushing your hair out so that it is tangle-free before you get it wet.

Pour the shampoo into your hand, and foam it up by rubbing your hands together. *Then* work the shampoo into your hair, scrubbing the scalp and being careful not to snarl the ends too much.

A good conditioner will help keep your hair healthy and will make it easier to untangle after shampooing. Keep a wide-toothed comb in the shower and comb through your hair *before* you rinse the conditioner out. Then rinse, being extra-careful not to snarl the ends.

Dry your hair carefully, and comb it out once more.

Untangling

Always use a wide-toothed comb to untangle your hair. Start with a small section of hair and comb out just the last few inches. Gradually work your way up this section until it is completely unsnarled, then start on another.

Parting

Draw a comb along the scalp where you want the part to be. Use your free hand to separate the two sections of hair.

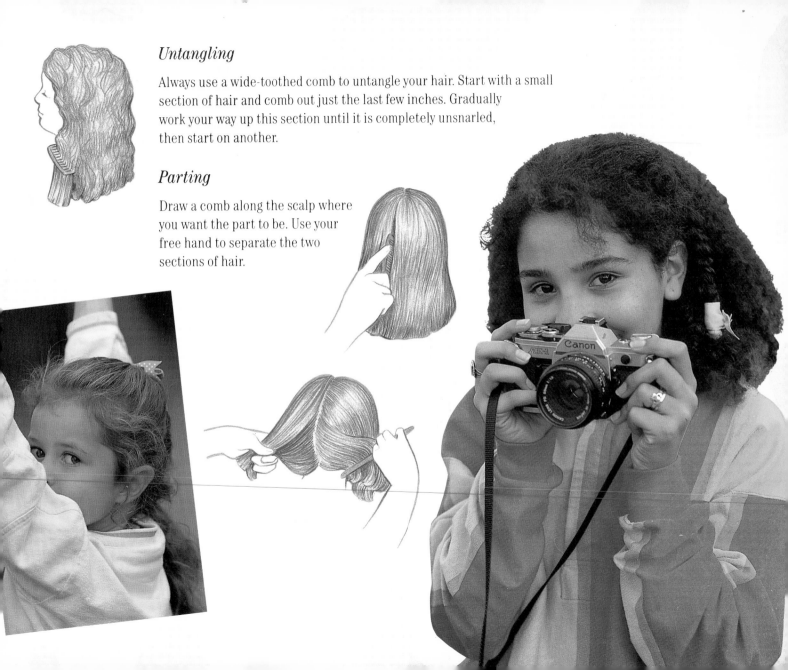

BASIC
Barrette Building

Stuff that comes with the book:

Wire

Barrette

Elastic band

We've provided most of what you'll need to make the bows in this book...

...though you will have to round up a needle and thread, some scissors, and clear fingernail polish.

You can find more blank barrettes at craft shops and good sewing supply stores.

Stuff you'll need to find:

Clear NAIL POLISH

Thread

Needle

Scissors

← Grosgrain

Satin →

Ribbons:

There are lots of different kinds of ribbons, but we've included two of the most common here: satin and grosgrain. The satin is the shiny stuff, which looks dressier. The grosgrain is the ribbon with the little ridges in it. It isn't as slippery as the satin ribbon and it's the same on both sides, so it is sometimes easier to work with. Any of the bows in this book can be made with either ribbon.

Paint a thin strip of clear fingernail polish on the ends of ribbon to keep them from unraveling. Be sure to let the polish dry completely before you start working with the ribbon. Your barrettes will last longer if you always finish the ribbon this way.

Clear NAIL POLISH

The Bow

The perfect hair bow is tied a little differently than the kind you would tie on your shoe. Use any ribbon you like: satin or velvet for something special, grosgrain for an everyday bow.

Cut the ends of your ribbon at an angle...

...or with two points.

1 Fold a ribbon around a ponytail or pigtail and tie it by crossing the right end over–then under–the left.

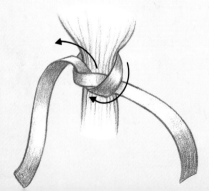

2 Pull the knot tight, then fold the ends into loops.

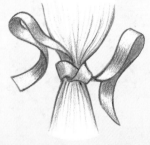

3 Now cross the left loop over–then under–the right loop...

4 ...and pull tight.

French-wired ribbon has wire running along the edges, so you can shape the bow any way you want and it will hold. Very nice.

5 Arrange the tails of the bow so they both hang down.

BASIC Styles

Pullbacks

Good for almost any length of hair.

The basic pullback is probably one of the easiest styles here. You can dress it up with a special bow, or keep it casual with a plain barrette.

Part the hair down the center. Pull it away from the face on both sides and clip it back with a barrette.

10

For a single pullback, part the hair on the side and clip one side back.

Twist Pullback

Same as the basic, except that before clipping the hair, twist it away from the face a few times.

11

Faux Bow

This is the easiest bow to put on a barrette. You can make it with one, two, or three loops.

1 Start with two pieces of ribbon that are each at least 8 inches long. Make one into a loop with its ends overlapping, and place it on a barrette.

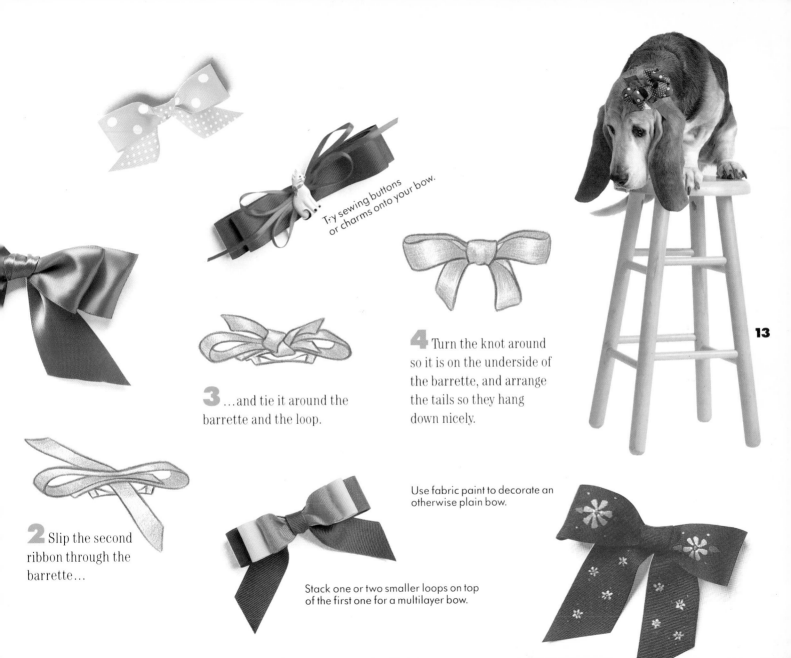

Try sewing buttons or charms onto your bow.

3 ...and tie it around the barrette and the loop.

4 Turn the knot around so it is on the underside of the barrette, and arrange the tails so they hang down nicely.

13

2 Slip the second ribbon through the barrette...

Use fabric paint to decorate an otherwise plain bow.

Stack one or two smaller loops on top of the first one for a multilayer bow.

T-shirt headband

You can make a great headband or ponytail holder by cutting the sleeves off an old T-shirt.

Cut the hemmed section off one sleeve, then cut off another strip about 2 inches wide to make a loop. Use this loop as a headband or a ponytail holder.

14

Headband

Good for any length of hair.

Try using a scarf, a bandana or even a man's tie instead of the ribbon.

Lift the hair out of the way and tie a ribbon in a square knot at the nape of the neck.

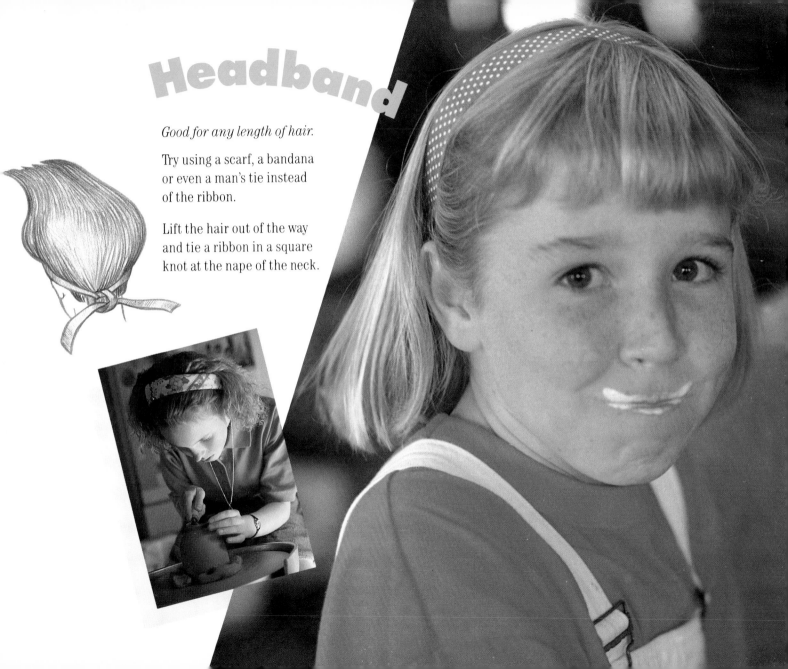

Pollyanna

Medium to long hair.

This style can be either very dressy
or completely casual, depending
on the barrette you use.

1

Starting at the ear on both
sides, gather the top layer
of hair...

2

...and hold it all together
in the back with an elastic
band or a barrette.

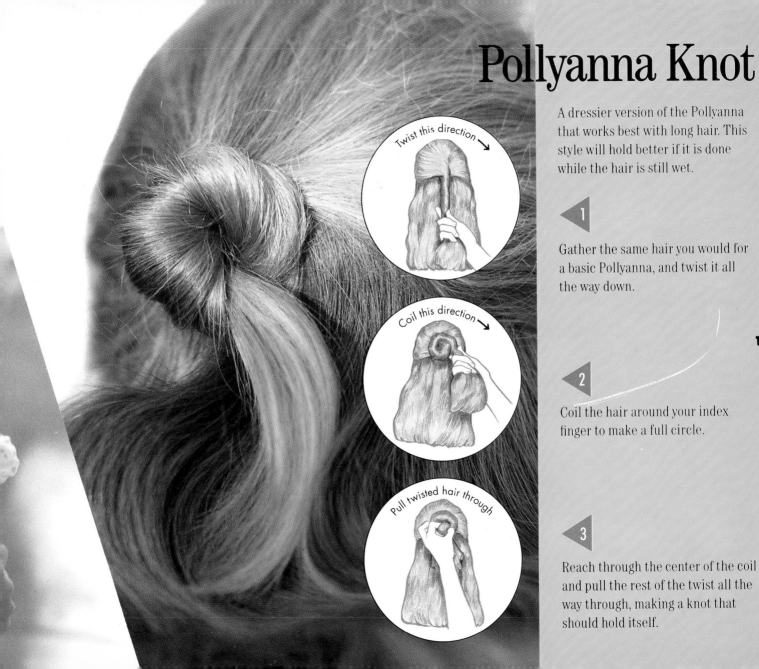

Pollyanna Knot

A dressier version of the Pollyanna that works best with long hair. This style will hold better if it is done while the hair is still wet.

 1

Gather the same hair you would for a basic Pollyanna, and twist it all the way down.

17

 2

Coil the hair around your index finger to make a full circle.

 3

Reach through the center of the coil and pull the rest of the twist all the way through, making a knot that should hold itself.

Twist this direction

Coil this direction

Pull twisted hair through

Ribbon Ruffle

A good bow for special occasions.

Using fingernail polish, finish the ends of one yard of 1½ inch wide satin ribbon. When the polish has dried, sew a line of stitches along one side of the ribbon as close to the edge as you can. Make the stitches about ¼ inch long.

Gather the ribbon so that it is twice the length of your barrette. Back-stitch once or twice to hold the gather, then tie off the thread.

Fold the ribbon into a "U" and sew along the gathered edge, joining the two halves.

Tie off and sew onto a medium or large barrette.

Balloony Bow

A fun barrette for parties.

All you need is a package of small balloons and a barrette.

Tie the balloons onto the barrette, alternating them so they point in a different direction each time.

Ponytail

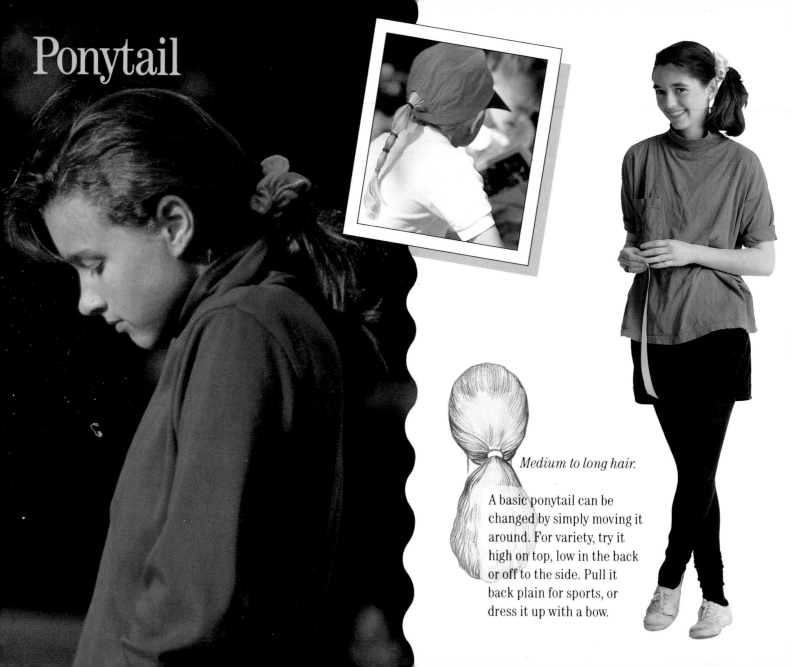

Medium to long hair.

A basic ponytail can be changed by simply moving it around. For variety, try it high on top, low in the back or off to the side. Pull it back plain for sports, or dress it up with a bow.

French Ponytail

Medium to long hair.

A cross between a Pollyanna and a ponytail. This is a good active style for medium to long hair, as it keeps the hair well off the face.

1 Gather the top layer of hair and secure high on the head with an elastic band, just as you would for a Pollyanna. (If you want a bow for this layer, tie it on now.)

2 Gather some more hair, combine it with the hair already banded, and secure with another elastic band. (Or another bow.)

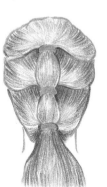

3 Gather the rest of the hair together and make one ponytail.

1

Make a tube by folding the fabric in half length-wise. The side that you want to show in the end (the right side) should be on the inside. Stitch along the edge.

right side

2

Pin a safety pin to one end, and push it back through the tube…

…to turn it right side out.

3

Take the pin off the tube and pin it to one end of the elastic. Thread it through the tube.

Scrunchie

A great way to hold ponytails, pigtails or Pollyannas. You can use just about any kind of fabric depending on whether you want an everyday scrunchie or something fancy.

You'll need a needle, thread, some elastic (approximately 8 inches long and ¼ inch wide) and a 4 x 24 inch piece of fabric.*

22

4 Be sure both ends of elastic stick out when you're done.

5 Tie the ends of the elastic in a strong knot.

6 Pull the ends of fabric together so they overlap, fold the top under, and stitch closed.

❋ If you want to use a scrunchie as a headband, you'll need a longer piece of elastic. Wrap the elastic around your head like a headband, and cut it to the length you want. You may want to cut the fabric a little longer, but not much.

pigtails

Good for almost any length of hair.

You can change the look of basic pigtails by moving them around. Don't worry if you can't catch all the hair in the pigtails. It looks fine even if some of the hair is left loose. This is an especially good style for sports.

24

Part the hair in the middle, all the way down the back of the head. Gather each side into a tail and secure with an elastic band.

How to make a Rosette

You can sew one rosette onto an elastic band, put a couple on a barrette, or sew a whole bouquet onto a scrunchie.

Start with a 24 inch long piece of ribbon that is at least one inch wide (wider is okay). Paint both ends with clear nail polish.

1 Fold one corner down as shown...

2 ...then sew a line of stitches all the way along one edge, catching the folded-down corner as you go.

3 Gather the ribbon tightly and tie off.

4 The pointy end of the ribbon is the center of the flower. Coil the ribbon around this end, and sew all the layers together from the bottom.

Sew finished rosette onto an elastic or a barrette.

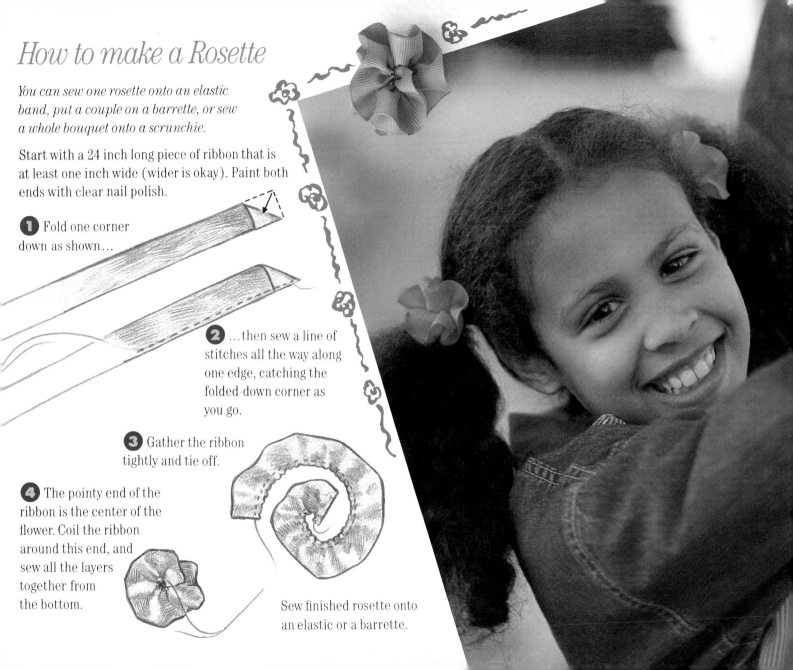

Flipthrough

Medium to long hair.

You can use this trick to
dress up a plain ponytail
or Pollyanna.

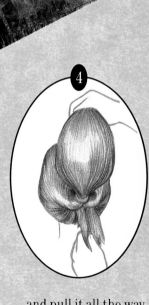

Start with a loose ponytail.

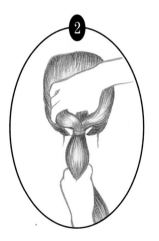

Reach down through the
hair above the elastic
band.

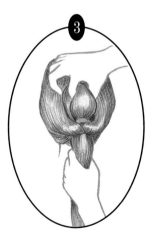

Grab the whole ponytail…

...and pull it all the way
through.

Basic *Bun*

Medium to long hair.
A classic style that can be used for dress-up occasions.

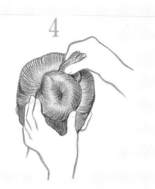

4

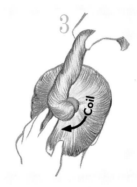

3

Coil

Tuck the end under the
outside coil…

…then coil the twist
around the elastic band.

5

2

Twist

Twist the entire ponytail…

…and secure with several
hair pins.*

1

Start with a ponytail.

* The pins will work best if they catch both the *underside*
of the bun and the hair closest to the head.

Loopies

You can use any kind of ribbon you like for this bow. Narrow, wide, grosgrain, satin: anything will work.

Use about 24 inches of wire, and one yard of ribbon. Paint the ends with nail polish as usual. Any size barrette will work.

① Fold the wire in half and attach to the barrette as shown. Twist the two wire ends together to make one strand.

Leave an inch of ribbon hanging.

② Wrap the wire around the ribbon to attach it to the barrette. Wide ribbon will get scrunched up, but that's fine.

③ Make ribbon loops, wrapping the wire around the barrette and ribbon to secure each one.

④ Tuck the end of the wire under the wire wraps, and trim it.

Loopy variations

1 Use 3–5 different colored ribbons. Sandwich them together and wire them onto the barrette…

2 …then spread them apart for a full party bow.

1 Wire two wide ribbons together, twisting the ribbon each time you make a loop. Spread the loops apart when you're finished wiring.

1 Tie a short piece of ribbon around the center of a loopy to make it look more like a bow.

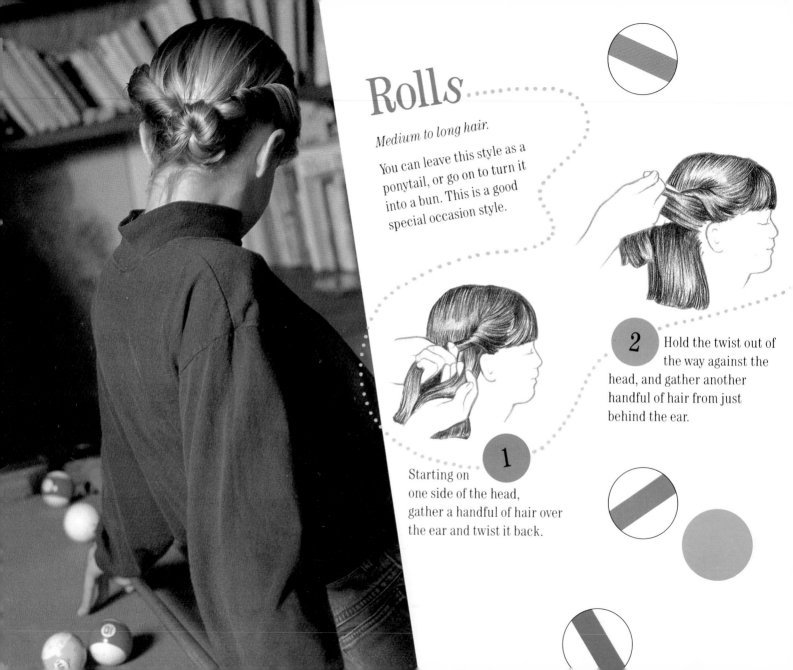

Rolls

Medium to long hair.

You can leave this style as a ponytail, or go on to turn it into a bun. This is a good special occasion style.

1 Starting on one side of the head, gather a handful of hair over the ear and twist it back.

2 Hold the twist out of the way against the head, and gather another handful of hair from just behind the ear.

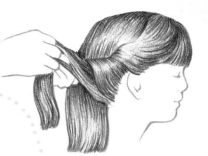

Roll

3

Add the new handful to the first twist and give the whole thing a few more twists.

4 Continue adding small handfuls of hair and twisting until...

5 ...all the hair on this side has been gathered into one big twist. Get your victim to hold it out of the way, as shown.

6 Do the same thing on the other side, then gather the two twists into a ponytail. Use an elastic band or a barrette to hold it.

BASIC

Braids

Basic Braid

Medium to long hair.

A ponytail braid is one of the best ways to keep your hair back during sports— even swimming.

1 Divide a ponytail into three strands.

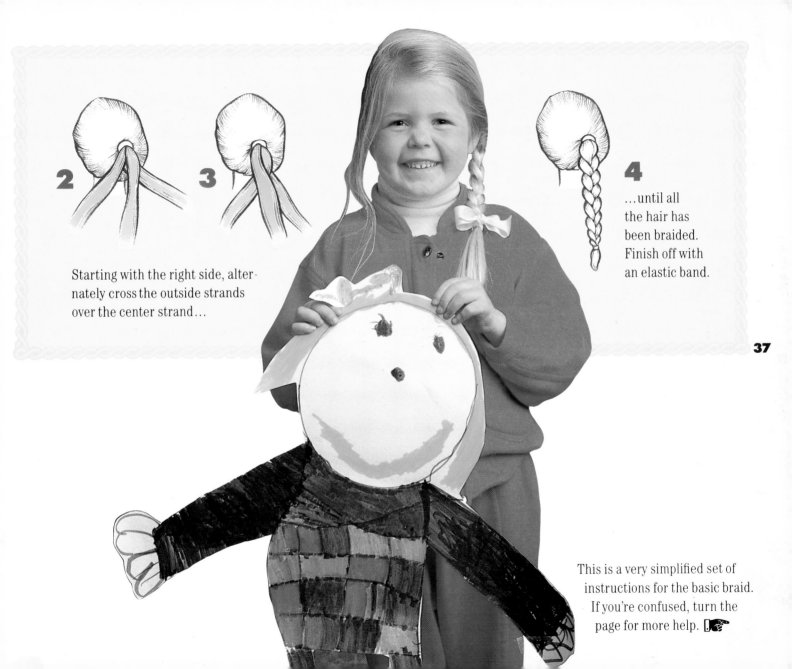

2 Starting with the right side, alternately cross the outside strands over the center strand…

3

4 …until all the hair has been braided. Finish off with an elastic band.

This is a very simplified set of instructions for the basic braid. If you're confused, turn the page for more help.

Basic Braid

If you need a little help coordinating
your hands, or if you want to learn
a really efficient way of braiding,
read on…

38

1 Divide a ponytail into
three sections and hold
as shown.

2 Roll the right hand
so that it is palm down.
This will cross the right
strand over the center.

3 Now move the center strand over to the left hand, holding the hair as shown.

4 Roll the left hand so that it is palm down. This will cross the left strand over the center.

5 Move the center strand back to your right hand and start over again from step 2.

Ribbon Braid

Long hair.

You can change a basic braid into something a little flashier by braiding a ribbon into it.

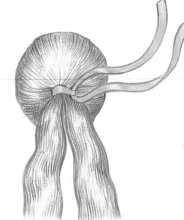

1 Tie a long ribbon around a ponytail and divide the ponytail into two strands.

2 The two tails of ribbon will be your third strand, so put them together and make sure they don't come apart. Now make a basic braid (page 36).

3 At the end of the braid, separate the ribbons…

4 …then wrap them around the end of the braid and tie off. You can just tie the ribbon in a knot, or make a bow if you want.

Divide a ponytail into three sections, and make each of those into an individual braid.

Add a nice detail to any style by making a tiny braid just behind the ear. Tie it off tightly using thread, and leave it in as long as it will stay—even during washings.

Braided Bun

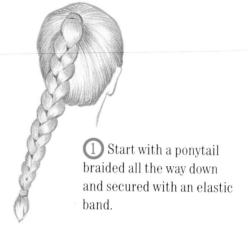

Long hair.

A variation on the basic bun. This is a great way to keep your hair out of the way, but still dressy.

① Start with a ponytail braided all the way down and secured with an elastic band.

Tuck end under

Coil

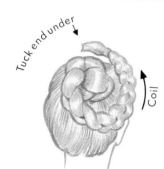

② Coil the pony-tail into a bun and hold it in place with hair pins.

Thumbelina

Long hair.

Make two high pigtails,
braid each one, then coil
them into buns. Pin in place.

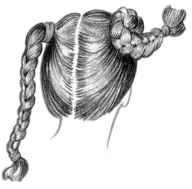

43

Caterpillar

This barrette can look very different depending on the width of ribbon you choose. It will work best if the ribbon is at least an inch wide.

1 Start with an 18 inch long piece of ribbon. Fold the ends under, and sew a line of big stitches all the way down the center. Be sure to catch the folded ends as you sew.

Fold ends under before you sew.

2 Gently pull the thread to gather the ribbon down to the length of the barrette you're using.

3 Take a few stitches to secure the gather, then tie the thread off.

Take a few stitches here.

4 Sew the gathered ribbon onto a medium-sized barrette.

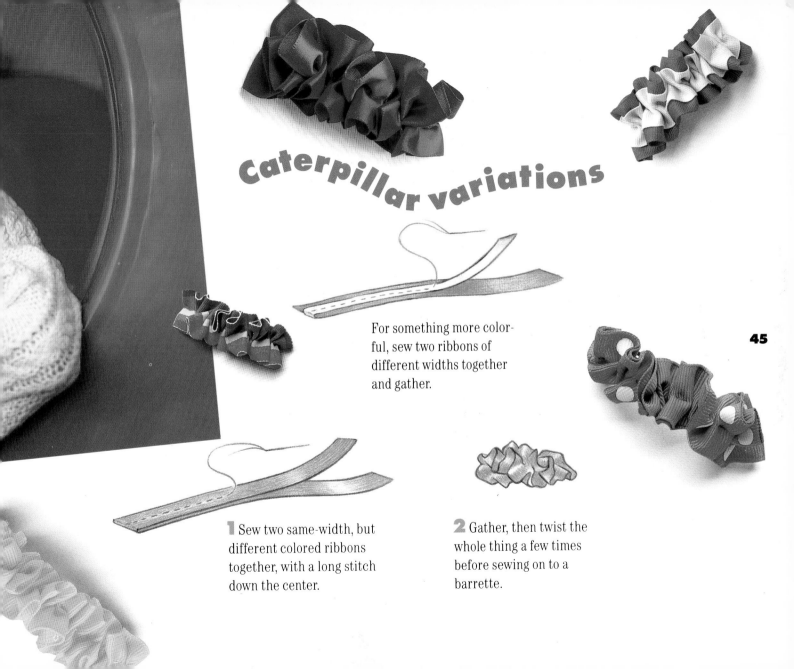

Caterpillar variations

For something more color-ful, sew two ribbons of different widths together and gather.

1 Sew two same-width, but different colored ribbons together, with a long stitch down the center.

2 Gather, then twist the whole thing a few times before sewing on to a barrette.

pigtail braid

Medium to long hair.

A simple style.
Great for sports.

1 Part the hair and gather it just as you would for a pigtail (page 24).

2 Divide each side into three strands and braid, starting with the piece of hair closest to the face.

← Start with this strand

3 Use an elastic band on the end of the braid.

For something a little different,
twist the first strand back
a few times before
braiding it with
the others.

47

Heidi Braids

Medium to long hair.

This is a good style for dress-up occasions. For something really special, you can poke fresh or dried flowers into the braid.

5 *Fresh Flowers*

Break off small flowers (any kind will do) so that their stems are about an inch long. Poke the stem all the way into the braid.

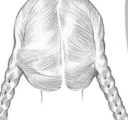

1 Start with basic pigtail braids (page 46).

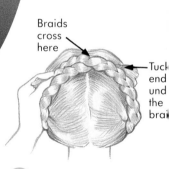

Braids cross here →

Tuck end und the brai

4 Wrap the second braid over the head, crossing over the first braid right at the top of the head. Pin in place.

2 Cross one pigtail over the top of the head and pin in place.

3 When pinning, try to catch the underside of the braid and some of the hair closest to the head.

Braided Tiara

Medium to long hair.

This style will work for hair that isn't quite long enough for a Heidi braid.

1 Pull a handful of hair back from each side of the face and braid it, starting just behind the ears.

2 Wrap the braids over the head just as you did for the Heidi braids. Pin in place.

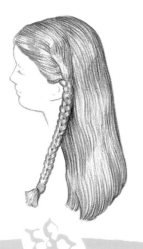

Leave the pouf plain, or sew a
rosette into the center.

Pouf

You'll need to round up some tulle netting (the kind tutus are made of) for this bow. You can find this at any fabric store. Cut about 14 strips that are 6 inches long and 2 inches wide. You can add a sparkle by twisting in strands of star wire (usually sold in gift-wrap stores).

Cover metal part

1 Tie net strips around an elastic band. Start by covering the metal part.

51

2 If you're using star wire, twist a piece onto the elastic after each piece of netting.

3 Continue tying on the netting and star wire, keeping it all bunched up together.

The Rope

Medium to long hair.

This is a pretty and unusual braid that looks much more difficult than it is. The rope will stay neater longer if you do it while the hair is still a little damp.

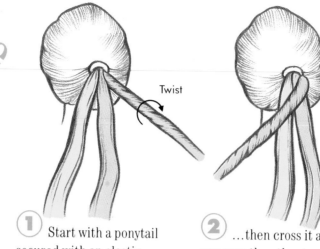

Twist

1 Start with a ponytail secured with an elastic band and divided into three sections. Twist the right section to the right several times...

2 ...then cross it all the way over the other two sections.

3 Repeat, always twisting the right strand to the right, and crossing it over the other two. Finish off with an elastic band when the braid is as long as you want it.

See facing page for more help. ➤

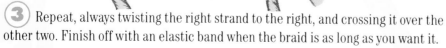

More Rope Instructions

If you're already roping hair with no problems, don't even read these instructions. If you get the idea, but don't seem to have enough hands to hold all the hair, this next section will give you a little more help.

You can make a tiny braid in your hair (page 41) and work it right into any other braid you like.

53

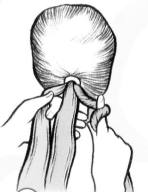

1 Divide a ponytail into three sections and hold as shown. Twist the right strand to the right by twirling it around your right forefinger.

Pinch here to keep hair twisted.

2 Move all the hair so it is held in the right hand like so…

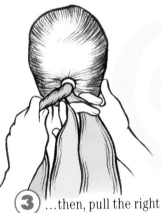

3 …then, pull the right strand across the other two strands…

4 …and hold as shown. Your right hand is free to twist the right strand again.

Repeat steps 1–4 until all the hair has been roped. Use an elastic band on the end.

Ponygirl Bow

This bow combines the loopy with a rosette.

1 Make a plain loopy using wide ribbon (page 30). Make a rosette out of a different colored ribbon (page 25).

2 Spread the loops apart as shown…

3 …then sew the rosette onto the center.

1

Make a ponytail and divide it in two.

Medium long to long hair.

This is a beautiful, special-occasion braid. The skinnier the strand of hair you use, the more intricate the braid will look.

2

Pull a skinny strand of hair out from *under* the right side and cross it over to join the left side.

Now pull a skinny strand of hair out from *under* the left side and cross it over to join the right side.

3

Repeat steps 2 and 3, always pulling a new strand from the underside of the braid.

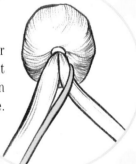

Turn the page if you need help.

More Fishtail

Skip this page if you don't need help coordinating your hands. But if you do…

1

Hold all the hair in the left hand as shown.

Move all the hair back to
the left hand.

Repeat steps 2–5 until the
braid is as long as you want
it. Be sure that you always
pull a new strand out from
under the braid.

2

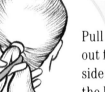

Pull a skinny strand of hair
out from under the right
side and cross it over to join
the left side.

4

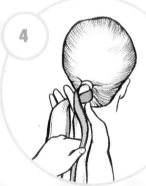

57

Now pull a skinny strand of
hair out from *under* the left
side, and cross it over to join
the right side. Tug down on
both strands to tighten
the braid.

3

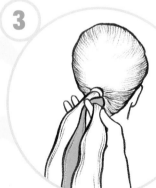

Move all the hair to the right
hand and hold as shown.

French

BRAIDS

French **Braid**

Medium to long hair.

This is a style you *must* learn. It's beautiful, simple, and it works as well in the pool as it does at the prom.

French braids are just like basic braids, except that you start with a small section of hair, and gradually add hair as you braid along.

What follows are instructions for the basic back-of-the-head French braid. Don't panic if it's not enough. Turn to page 62 for the real, hands-on instructions.

Gather a handful of hair from the top of the head and divide it into three strands. Cross first the right—then the left—over the center as if you were starting a basic braid.

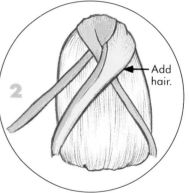

Add some new hair to the right strand to make one bigger strand. Cross the whole thing over the center.

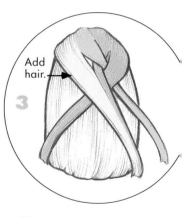

Now add some hair to the left strand and cross it over the center.

Repeat steps 2 and 3 until all the hair has been added into the braid then finish off with a basic braid. Use an elastic band on the end.

French Braid Basics

Gathering Hair

Start by gathering a section of hair 2–3 inches wide.

Gather hair like this…

…not this.

Adding Hair

For the basic back-of-the-head French braid, use your fingernail to make a part and draw a section of hair back from the face to the braid.

For an intricate, more formal braid, add skinny strands of hair. For a more active, informal braid, add fat strands. In either case, try to be consistent.

Keeping the Braid Tight

Always work with your hands close to the head. In fact, go ahead and press your hands right up against the head as you braid.

Anytime you find yourself holding all the hair in one hand, use your free hand to tug down on the strands, tightening the braid.

If you need a little more help...

These instructions are written especially for people who, like you, have only two hands. Take a big breath and read on. You'll do fine.

62

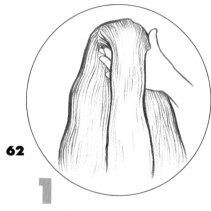

1

Start by gathering a handful of hair from the top of the head. Easy.

2

Divide this section into three strands and cross the right–then the left–over the center (just like a basic braid). Hold all the hair in the left hand as shown.

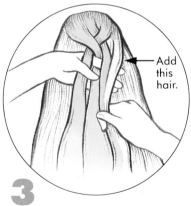

← Add this hair.

3

Pull a small section of hair back from the right side of the face and add it to the right strand...

4

...then pull the center strand all the way to the right...

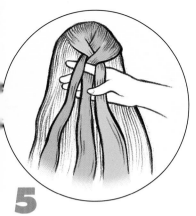

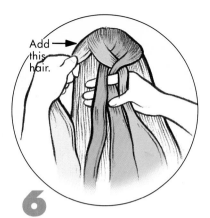

5 ...and move all the hair to the right hand as shown. This is a good time to pull the strands down with your free hand to tighten the braid.

6 Now add more hair to the left strand. Be sure to keep your hands close to the head.

Add this hair.

7 Pull the center strand all the way to the left...

63

8 ...and hold all the hair in the left hand. Again, pull the strands down with your free hand to tighten the braid.

Repeat steps 3–8 until all the hair has been caught up in the braid. Finish off with a basic braid.

Don't expect your first (or your second) French braid to look right. It takes a little practice to keep the braid snug and neat.

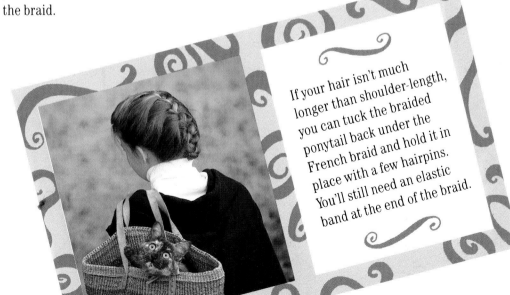

If your hair isn't much longer than shoulder-length, you can tuck the braided ponytail back under the French braid and hold it in place with a few hairpins. You'll still need an elastic band at the end of the braid.

Medium to long hair.

A great active style for anyone who's mastered the French braid. You'll use all the same techniques; the hair is simply braided on each side instead of down the back.

These directions are for the right side. To braid on the left side, substitute the word *left* every time you see the word right, and vice versa.

1 Part the hair all the way down the center just as you would for a pigtail. Gather a section of hair that runs from just in front of the ear all the way up to the center part.

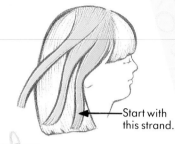

Start with this strand.

2 Divide this section into three pieces.

3 Now start just as you would if you were making a basic pigtail braid: cross the right strand–then the left strand–over the center.

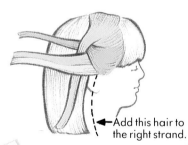

Add this hair to the right strand.

4 Pull a small section of hair up from the ear, and add it to the *right* strand. Cross the now-bigger *right* strand over the center.

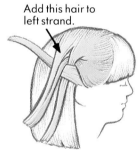

Add this hair to left strand.

5 Pull another section of hair down from the center part and add it to the left strand. Cross the now-bigger left strand over the center.

Repeat steps 4 and 5 until all the hair on this side of the head has been caught up in the braid, then continue with a basic braid. Use an elastic band at the end.

Princess **Anne** Braid

1 Start with French pigtails. French braid the first side just until you've caught all the hair in the braid. Use an elastic band to hold it while you braid the second side.

Long hair.

This is a beautiful and intricate-looking braid which can be worn almost anytime. It's based on French pigtails, so be sure you know how to make those first.

2 When you've completed both French braids, take the elastic band off the first one and hold one braid in each hand exactly as shown. Be sure the braids on *each* side end with the right strand crossing over the center.

3 Now roll your right hand over and transfer all the hair in that hand to the left hand, combining the six strands into three. The hair that was between the thumb and first finger on the right hand will now be added to the hair between the thumb and first finger of the left hand, and so on.

4 Using your now-free right hand, pull the hair tight, then continue with a basic braid. Start by crossing the right strand over the center. This should work fine as long as you were careful to finish *both* pigtails by crossing the right strand over the center. Secure with an elastic band as usual.

An elegant variation on the Ribbon Ruffle. Use one ribbon, or two different-colored ribbons. In either case, satin ribbon will ripple in the nicest way.

the **ripple**

1 Start with a piece of satin ribbon that is 18 inches long and at least 1½ inches wide. If you're using two ribbons, cut them to the same length and place them back to back . Finish the ends with clear nail polish.

2 Whether you're using one ribbon or two, the next step is the same. Sew along the very edge of the ribbon. If you're working with two ribbons, this will join them.

3 Now gather the ribbon until it is the length of your barrette. Take a few stitches at the end so the ribbon stays gathered, and tie it off.

4 Arrange the ruffle as shown and sew onto a barrette.

French OVER

Medium to long hair.

This is a good everyday style that can be dressed up with a pretty bow or flowers for special events. Be sure you are comfortable with the basic French braid before you try it.

1 Using a comb to make a clean part, separate out a section of hair running from just behind one ear all the way over the head to the other.

2 Start braiding close to the first ear, continuing with a French braid that runs all the way over the head.

3 Once all the hair in this section has been French braided, finish up with a basic braid and secure it with an elastic band.

CONFETTI bow

You'll need some curling ribbon for this barrette. This is a special kind of ribbon you can get just about anywhere gift wrap is sold. Use as many different colors as you like.

1 Cut the ribbon into pieces about 15 inches long. Tie each piece of ribbon around the barrette as shown. Tie on enough to completely cover the barrette.

2 Curl the ribbon using a butter knife (nothing sharp!). Starting close to the barrette, pinch the ribbon between your thumb and the knife and pull the knife all the way out to the end of the ribbon.

INSIDE-OUT French braid

Medium to long hair.

The inside-out braid is just like a French braid, except it's done in reverse. The outside strands cross *under* the center strand, not *over*. You can use the inside-out French braid anytime you would use the regular French braid.

A cornrow is a lot of little French braids (regular or inside-out) running all over the head. You can make cornrows with almost any kind of hair, but be prepared, it's a lot of work.

Instructions are on the next page.

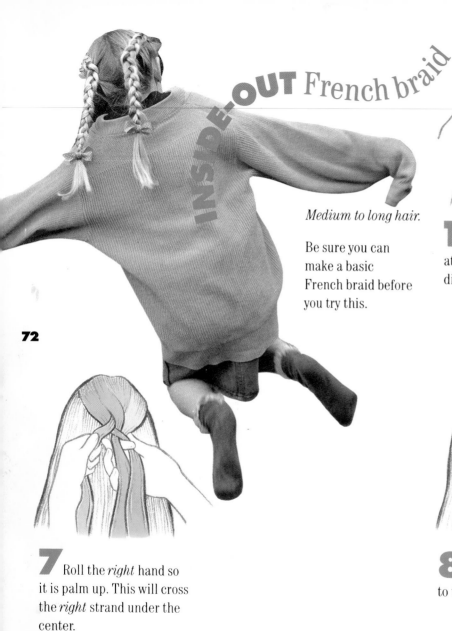

Medium to long hair.

Be sure you can make a basic French braid before you try this.

72

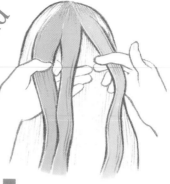

1 Gather a section of hair at the top of the head and divide it into three sections.

2 Cross the right strand *under* the center…

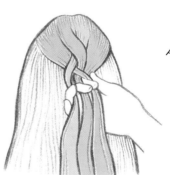

7 Roll the *right* hand so it is palm up. This will cross the *right* strand under the center.

8 Now move all the hair to the right hand…

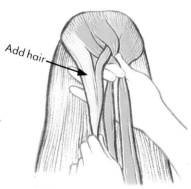

Add hair

9 …and add some hair to the left strand.

 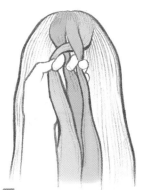 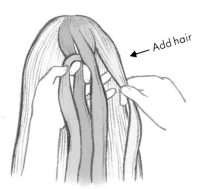 

Add hair →

3 …then cross the left strand *under* the center.

4 Hold all the hair in the left hand as shown.

5 Add some hair to the right strand…

6 …then grab the right and *center* strand with the right hand as shown.

73

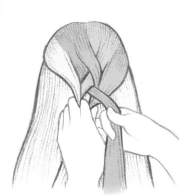 

10 Grab the *left* and *center* strands with the *left* hand as shown…

11 …and roll the left hand so it is palm up, crossing the left strand under the center.

Repeat steps 4–11 until all the hair has been worked into the braid. Continue with a basic inside-out braid, always crossing the outside strands of hair *under* the center strand. Use an elastic band on the end.

Rosette with leaf

1 ੨ੳ

Start with a piece of 1 inch wide green ribbon that is about 7 inches long. Loop it into a circle so that its ends overlap.

2 ੨ੳ

Wrap a piece of thread around the middle several times, pulling it tight so the ribbon bunches up. It should look something like a bow. Tie the thread in a sturdy knot.

3 ੨ੳ

Tie another piece of thread at the end of each loop of the bow, pull tight, and tie off.

4 ੨ੳ

Make a rosette out of 1 inch wide ribbon (page 25) and sew it to the center of the leaf. Sew the whole thing onto a barrette, an elastic band, or a headband.

 # Rope

Medium to long hair.

Tricky, but a beautiful braid. Prerequisites: Basic rope (page 52) and the French braid (page 60). This page has the basic idea, the pages that follow have more detailed instructions.

1

Gather a handful of hair at the top of the head as you would for a French braid. Divide it into three pieces. Cross the right–then the left–over the center, as if you were starting a basic braid.

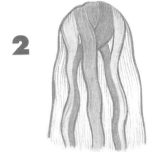

2

Now add a little hair to *both* the left and the right strands.

3

Twist both of these strands to the *right*...

4

...and cross the right strand over the other two.

Repeat steps 2–4 until all the hair has been roped. Continue to braid the rest of the hair in a basic rope.

Turn to the next page if you need more help. ➡

More Help with the *French* Rope

If you're reading this, it's probably because you're having trouble holding all the hair and keeping it twisted. This next section will help. As always, if you've already figured out a good way to hold the hair, skip this page.

Don't worry if this doesn't look right at first. You have to work pretty far down the head before it really starts to look like a rope.

1 Start just as you would for a French braid: gather a handful of hair from the top of the head, divide it in three, and cross first the right—then the left—strand over the center.

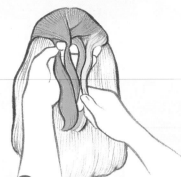

2 Hold all the hair in the *left* hand as shown, and add a little hair to the *right* strand.

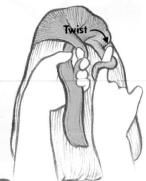

Twist

3 Use your right hand to twist the *right* strand to the right.

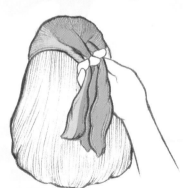

6 *...then twist this strand* to the right and hold as illustrated.

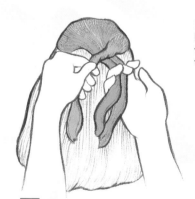

7 Using your left hand, pick up the twisted right strand and pull it all the way over the other two strands.

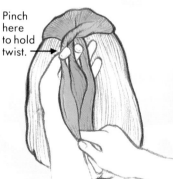

Pinch here to hold twist.

8 Move the rest of the hair over to the left hand.

4 Now move all the hair to the *right* hand, pinching the twist so it doesn't unwind.

5 Add some hair to the left…

Repeat steps 2–8 until you reach the nape of the neck and all the hair has been caught up in the rope. Continue with a basic rope and finish off with an elastic band.

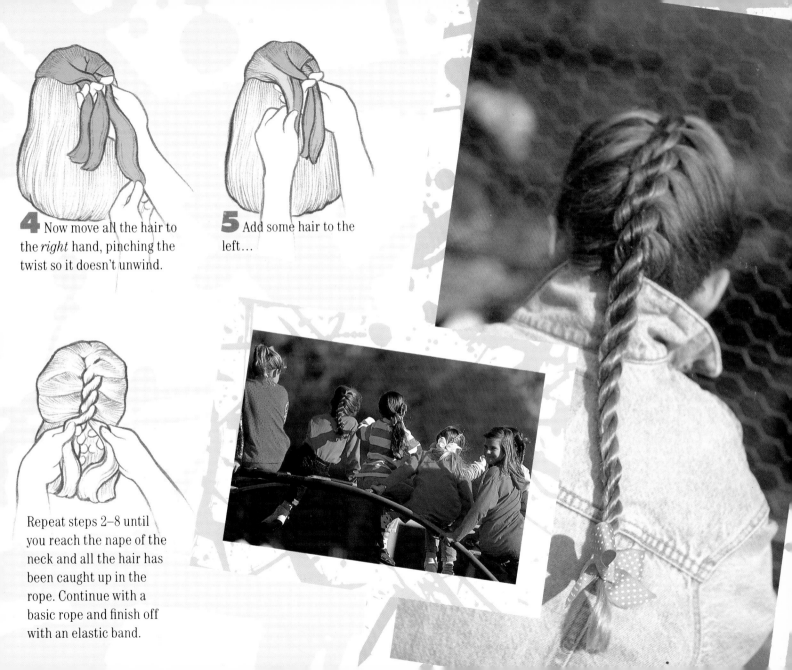

Wreaths

Floral wreaths are a beautiful way to dress up any hairstyle for a really special occasion. You can start with fresh or dried flowers–either will work fine. Statice and baby's breath are always a good choice as they will dry nicely on a wreath, but feel free to experiment with whatever flowers you happen to like or have around.

You'll need to round up a few extra supplies: green floral tape and a piece of floral wire (usually around 18 inches long). You can buy these at a craft store or pick them up at any florist's shop. And of course you'll need a bunch of pretty flowers.

1 Bend the ends of the wire back to make hooks. Wrap the tape around one hook, so that the end is completely covered, then wrap it around the wire a few times.

2 Break a flower off your bunch, leaving about 1 inch of stem. Lay it along the wire with the stem pointing to the unfinished end. Wrap the floral tape around the stem and the wire.

3 Continue adding flowers, all pointing in the same direction, and wrapping the tape around their stems, until you've completely covered the wire with flowers. Wrap the tape around the wire a few times then trim it. Leave the hook free on this end.

4 Make the wire into a circle and link the hook with the loop on the other end.

If you've made a fresh wreath and want to dry it, hang it in a cool, dry place for a couple of days.

The Kids' Credits

The following kids and teens lent us their happy faces to appear in our book. We'd like to thank them one and all by name.

Fu-sang Yin, Justine Wool, James Wheatley, Sara Watts, Felicia Walker, Allison Van Loo, Haruka Uchiyama, Kirsten Tobey, Jessica Thomas, Frida Suro, Molly Street, Merissa Smith, Latanya Smith, Kristine Simons, Emily Schuman, Rosie the Bassett, Rikkia Robinson, Leah Robinson, Camila Reynolds, Abigail Reider, Hana Raftery, Lizabeth Pollack, Maren Pearson, Laura Pearson, Jenny Parsells, Ashleigh Parsells, Vickie Nguyen, Zania Musson, Ninel Musson, Katy Murphy, Heather Murphy, Amber Mortensen, Kasey Moore, Allyssa Mitchell, Kate Milroy, Kadia Usmano Martin, Sara Martens, Stephanie Lundin, Christina Loarie, London Lawler, Sharon Lau, Abby Kojola, Anne Johnson, Melissa Jensen, Anne Jensen, Meredith Horiuchi, Liz Holmes, Michelle Hoag, Katie Herzog, Georgia Rae Herzog, Rachel Hamilton, Jenna Hamilton, Beckett Haight, Faith Goss, Jessica Ginsburg, Amy Griffin, Kate Gallagher, Leslie Fuller, Lindsay Frankfurt, Whitton Frank, Naomi Frank, Kristin Fowler, Jennifer Foster, Katie Fleishman, Sophia Englert, Kristin Engel, Robin Easterbrook, Meredith Dunton, Elisabeth Dornbrach, Catherine Digovich, Elizabeth Dietrich, Lauren Dey, Katherine Dey, Bruna Delgado, Jennifer Cady, Katie Brizgys, Molly Brizgys, Erica Breese, Allison Bird, Kari Bell, Sarah Beebe, Heide Beck, Katherine Bechtel, Brendan Bechtel, Kristin Beaver, Brenda Batton, Jhumki Basu, Tori Barber, Kari Barber.

The Grown-Ups' Credits

Principal photographers: Peter Fox, Thomas Heinser and Jock McDonald. David Peterson, Kim Raftery and Ed Young also contributed. Fish photo on page 55–56 by F. Stuart Westmorland/ Allstock. *Hair Styling and Braiding:* Anne Johnson, Robin Stoneking, Victor Hutchins, Sheila Jurden, and Sharil Stevenson. Lisa Andreonie and Katje Sabin-Newmiller consulted. All the Klutzniks, especially Jo Janke, Kathy Gilmartin and Estela Fernandez, were hair victims. Kim Raftery coordinated most of the logistics and casting. John Cassidy interfered throughout. Locations were provided through the courtesy of the Palo Alto Unified School District, and Escondido, Juana Briones, and Duveneck Elementary Schools.

Additional help and locations were provided by: The Palo Alto Cultural Center, the Palo Alto Children's Library, Hidden Villa Ranch, the Elizabeth F. Gamble Garden Center, Stanford University, Castilleja School, Peninsula Fountain and Grill, Menlo Academy of Dance, Winterland Lodge, Dottie Doolittle Clothing, and Jylene Specialty Flowers. In a particularly personal sacrifice, Wendy Dey, Susan Rosenberg, Kathy Felix, Polly Pollack and Marde Ross temporarily deeded over their homes for the cause.

For More Information About Klutz Press Publications

Please send for our free mail order catalogue.

Klutz Press
2121 Staunton Court
Palo Alto, CA 94306
tel. (415) 424-0739